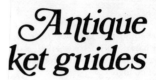

Antique
ket guides

TEA CADDIES

by

Noël Riley

Series Editor: Noël Riley

SEVEN HILLS BOOKS
Cincinnati

LUTTERWORTH PRESS
Cambridge

Cover illustration shows: *Top right:* a satinwood tea caddy
with oval marquetry reserves, elaborate stringing lines and
marquetry flutes on the front canted corners; English, *c.*1785,
4¾ in. high.
Top left: an octagonal filigree paperwork tea caddy of *c.*1780,
4¾ in. high.
Centre: a rare octagonal caddy decorated with black and gold
japanning and ivory stringing lines, English *c.*1780, 4 in. high.
Lower right: a fruitwood tea caddy in the form of an apple,
English *c.*1800, 4½ in. high.
Lower left: a small tea caddy veneered in red tortoiseshell
with ivory stringing lines and with its own tortoiseshell
piqué caddy spoon inside, English, *c.*1790, 3¼ in. high.
Photograph courtesy of Asprey and Co., London, W.1.

**First published in 1985 by Lutterworth Press,
7 All Saints' Passage, Cambridge CB2 3LS.**
U.K. ISBN 0-7188-2598-5

Published in the United States by Seven Hills Books,
519 West Third Street, Cincinnati, Oh. 45202.
U.S. ISBN 0-911403-25-6

Photoset by Nene Phototypesetters Ltd, Northampton

Printed and bound in Great Britain by
Butler & Tanner Ltd, Frome and London

Contents

1. *An English Family at Tea*, *c.*1720, oil on canvas by Joseph van Aken (*c.*1700–1749). Tea caddies and case rest at corner of carpet.

Introduction

TEA drinking is known to have been fashionable in China as early as the T'ang Dynasty (618–906 AD) and by the ninth century the Japanese had taken up and ritualized the habit. However, it was not until the early 17th century that tea reached Europe: merchant adventurers brought it to Holland around 1610 and by the 1650s it was being sold in England.

The tea plant is a variety of the camellia and its leaves go through various processes of drying, rolling and sometimes fermenting before being blended and packed for consumption. These methods have remained essentially the same for hundreds of years. When the tea leaves are fermented before being dried the resulting tea is known as black or bohea. Unfermented leaves make green, or hyson, tea. Nowadays mostly we drink black tea, but in the 17th and 18th centuries green tea was nearly as popular although more expensive.

The high cost of tea made it at first available only to the rich, and at the same time conferred a social cachet which was further enhanced by the example of Charles II's queen, Catherine of Braganza, an enthusiastic tea drinker. It is hard now to appreciate just how very expensive tea was to the 17th and 18th century citizen. In 1665 Thomas Garway, one of the first English tea dealers, advertised tea for sale from 16s.–50s. per lb, and in 1716 Thomas Twining was selling tea for around 16s. per lb at his coffee house in the Strand. This represents about £65 in present-day currency. Heavy import duties as well as the East India Company's monopoly for importing tea (which was not lifted until 1833) kept the price artificially high for most of the 18th century and widespread smuggling was a result. It has been estimated that as much tea was smuggled as was legally imported, and buying smuggled

2. A selection of tea caddies, *left to right:* late 18th century satinwood crossbanded and inlaid on the front with a patera; Regency period tortoiseshell chest with silver inlays, feet and finial; late 18th century ivory with cut steel bead decoration and inset Wedgwood medallion; a late 18th century English fruitwood melon; late 18th century tortoiseshell with ivory fillets and an inset miniature painting, and an Adam period oval decorated with birds on a tree and borders of marquetry.

tea was considered perfectly respectable. Even the moderate Parson Woodforde of Norfolk mentions his account 'to one Richard Andrews a Smuggler for a Pound of 9s Tea' in 1777. Tea was also adulterated with other leaves to make it go further, and in spite of severe penalties for those found at it, the practice was widespread. Vigorous campaigning by the legitimate tea trade to reduce tea taxes eventually resulted in the Commutation Act of 1784 which effectively halved the price of tea.

Long before this, however, tea had spread down the social scale: tea was often a primary consideration in servants' wages. In 1776, for example, Parson Woodforde took on a maid for five guineas a year 'and tea twice daily.' As early as 1751 Charles Deering, recording tea drinking habits in Nottingham, remarked 'The people here are not without their Tea, Coffee and Chocolate, especially the first, the Use of which is spread to that Degree that not only the Gentry and Wealthy Traders drink it constantly, but almost every Seamer, Sizer and Winder will have her Tea and will enjoy herself over it in a morning'. During the second half of the 18th century English tea consumption has been estimated as at least one cup per head of population per day.

Not surprisingly, many people regarded tea as ruinous to the poor, and not only for economic reasons. While its medicinal qualities were applauded in some quarters it was decried as a heathen brew, full of 'corrosive,

gnawing and poisonous powers' in others. But tea drinking was firmly established among rich and poor alike. Only the rich, however, could afford the expensive accoutrements which went with the elegant ritual of drawing-room tea drinking. From the late 17th century onwards these had included containers for dry tea leaves.

The earliest tea caddies were bottle-shaped vessels made, like their contemporary tea bowls and saucers, of porcelain imported from China, and the tea was measured out at the table from their cup-shaped lids. They were in fact known as tea bottles or tea jars, the word caddy being adopted much later, towards the end of the 18th century. The word comes from the Malay/Chinese word *Kati*, denoting a measure of tea weighing about 1⅓ lbs, and the single-compartment wooden boxes holding approximately this weight and made from the 1780s onwards were the first to become known as tea caddies.

From the early 18th century lockable trunk-shaped tea boxes were known as tea chests, and this was the term generally used until the late 18th century. Each chest would contain a set of two or three canisters – of wood, pewter, silver, enamel or glass. The lids of these inner canisters were tightly fitted to protect the tea from damp and insects; some were hinged, some were sliding and others consisted of caps which fitted neatly over collars.

While the two outer canisters in a set of three were for two different kinds of tea

7

(usually green and black) it is now generally accepted that the middle container (which is often of a different size) was for sugar, another expensive commodity. Dean Swift, writing in 1729, refers to 'small chests and trunks, with lock and key, wherein they keep the tea and sugar'. Later, this middle vessel most commonly took the form of a glass bowl. The *Cabinet-Makers' London Book of Prices* (1793) gives prices for the internal fittings of tea chests and these include 'a hole cut to receive the sugar bason' and 'making a case for the sugar-bason to lift out'.

During the second half of the 18th century tea chests and caddies were made in prodigious variety. Whereas during the 1750s and 60s the finest were made of silver, enamel, porcelain or mahogany, by the 1780s other materials such as ivory, tortoiseshell, mother-of-pearl, glass, filigree paper, papier mâché and many exotic woods were also being used. The shapes of caddies showed similar diversity. By the 19th century wood was the dominant material for tea caddies, with porcelain and silver examples being rarely produced.

Although tea caddies continued to be made throughout the 19th century there was a gradual decline in their use, almost certainly because of a shift in social habits. Once tea had ceased being the exotic and expensive commodity it had been until the 1830s (the East India Company's monopoly for importing tea into England was lifted in 1833, and Indian-grown tea was imported from 1839), the tea leaves were no longer kept in the drawing room to be measured out by the lady of the house. Tea was now made in the kitchen and was served, ready brewed, in the teapot.

Tea caddies of the 18th and early 19th century not only reflect an important and fascinating social custom, but they demonstrate the best craftsmanship in practically every decorative material and technique of the age. It is probably this, together with their endless variety, that makes them so attractive to collectors (fig. 2).

1. Pottery and Porcelain

3. A Meissen tea caddy and cover of baluster form and hexagonal section painted by J. G. Höroldt with panels of chinoiserie figures divided by gilt borders, *c.*1725–30. This was sold by Sotheby Parke Bernet for £7,150 in 1983.

4. *(below)* Square bottle-shaped Meissen caddy with Kakiemon decoration and metal (replacement) lid, *c.*1730–35.

LATE 17th century tea drinkers had to rely almost exclusively on Chinese imports for their tea equipage. These included blue and white porcelain and also the hard red stonewares of Yi Hsing. They were used for tea bowls and saucers as well as teapots, and for the tea jars of globular or flat-sided bottle shape, which were brought to the table and from whose lids the tea leaves were measured (fig. 1).

By the last years of the 17th century potters in England such as John Dwight of Fulham and the Elers brothers were making red stoneware in imitation of the Chinese, and a similar hard red stoneware was produced by Johann-Friedrich Böttger at Meissen from 1707; this was the main stepping stone in the European

5. Höchst porcelain tea caddy with figure decoration by Öttner, c.1760.

6. *(below)* First period Worcester ovoid fluted tea caddy painted with the jabberwocky pattern in bright turquoise and iron red, c.1770. The ovoid is a typically English shape.

re-discovery of Chinese or true porcelain a year later. By the 1720s the Meissen porcelain factory was producing beautifully painted porcelain tea jars both of globular form and the flat-sided, shouldered bottle shape, to go with the tea sets that only the very rich could afford (figs. 3 and 4). They were copied by other European factories such as Vezzi in Venice and du Paquier in Vienna in the 1720s and 30s, and later, in the 1760s and 70s, at German factories such as Ludwigsburg and Fürstenberg and at the Worcester factory in England (figs. 5, 6 and 7).

A great number of potteries from the 1740s onwards produced tea jars. They come in a fascinating range of shapes from square, rec-

7. A pair of tea jars decorated on-glaze with apple-green grounds and painted by the so-called 'spotted fruit painter', Worcester, c.1770–80.

tangular or octagonal boxes, to fanciful shapes like pineapples, cauliflowers or human figures, and were made in most of the ceramic bodies of the time (fig. 8). Of a similar class were the Lowestoft soft-paste porcelains, designed, like the pottery wares, for a less opulent market than the fine porcelains of Worcester, and tea canisters with underglaze blue and moulded decoration were produced in the 1760s (fig. 9).

8. *(below – left to right)* Staffordshire earthenware tea caddy dated 1796, decorated in underglaze blue; Prattware caddy, c.1790, and an earthenware canister moulded on each side with either a seated chinaman or a standing chinese lady, and covered with a tortoiseshell glaze, Whieldon or Whieldon type, c.1755–60.

9. Lowestoft blue and white underglaze printed square tea bottle with a flower knob on the lid, *c*.1770–75.

Chinese blue and white porcelain tea bottles were still being imported; many of their designs followed English prints and some were embellished with gilding in English workshops on their way to the retailers, no doubt to give a grander appearance (and a higher price) to a long familiar form. More status-enhancing were the Chinese armorial wares, decorated with polychrome flowers and armorials and with gilding, that were imported to Europe for most of the 18th century.

Glass

THE subject of glass tea caddies is a somewhat contentious one because of the inevitable confusion about the original purpose of various glass vessels – both of box and of bottle shape – which could have been used for storing tea but which may also have been intended for sugar, tobacco, spirits or the toilet table (figs. 10 and 11). Happily, no confusion exists with regard to the well-known pairs of opaque white glass bottles with enamel caps mounted in gilt copper which were probably made in South Staffordshire 1755–60. They are decorated with finely painted flowers and birds in enamel colours and one is labelled 'Green' and the other 'Bohea' (fig. 12). Occasionally a transparent glass bottle is similarly labelled, giving weight to the theory that others may have been made as tea caddies too.

Most glass tea canisters were made in sets

10. *(above)* Slender tea bottle of dark green glass cut with flat flutes and fitted with its original tortoiseshell piqué cover, English, *c.*1740–50.
11. *(below)* Inlaid satinwood tea caddy fitted with a pair of oval glass bottles cut with flat geometric patterns and fitted with engraved silver covers, *c.*1770–75.

to fit into chests; many follow closely the designs and shapes of silver examples, and some are silver mounted (fig. 13). A notice in the *London Chronicle* in December 1766 refers to 'Several Sets of silver mounted blue glass Tea Canisters in Shagreen Chests,' which may well have been of the Bristol type. From the 1760s onwards glass boxes of rectangular, square or oval shape and cut with star and other patterns were also made. Most have

12. *(above)* Pair of tea bottles of opaque-white glass painted with finches and flowers in natural colours by the so-called 'swirled flower painter', labelled 'Green' and 'Bohea', and fitted with their original gilt metal and Staffordshire enamel covers, *c*.1755–60.

13. *(right)* Set of three silver-mounted tea canisters of cut glass, closely following silver shapes, and fitted into a silver-mounted shagreen chest complete with sugar nips, mote spoon and teaspoons. It was given to Sir Joshua Reynolds in 1768.

14. A pair of tea caddies of blue cut glass fitted with heavy cast silver mouldings and set in a tortoiseshell box with silver mounts, English, *c*.1765.

14

15. Set of oval tea jars and a sugar box cut with the so-called hoops and staves pattern which originated *c*.1775. These jars, with their silver lids by William Kingdon, were probably made *c*.1810.

16. Three cut glass tea boxes with ormolu mounts of high quality, French, *c*.1815–20.

decorative gilt metal or silver mounts and finials and when these are hallmarked they can be dated fairly precisely (figs. 14 and 15).

Early 19th century glass tea boxes were generally oval, square, rectangular or octagonal, with beautifully cut all-over patterns and decorative metal mounts. They were made in France and Ireland as well as England. French examples can generally be distinguished by the quality of their elaborately patterned ormolu mounts (fig. 16), while Irish glass caddies are usually mounted in base metals engraved with charmingly simple bright-cut patterns (figs. 17 and 18). The cutting on Irish glass is generally of a softer quality than that of English (figs. 19 and 20). From Bohemia come early 19th century white milk glass tea boxes with gilt metal mounts, sometimes decorated with views of watering places or picturesque landscapes.

17. *(top left)* Small Irish tea box of oblong form with canted corners and cut hollow flutes and festoons, *c.*1790.

18. *(top right)* A tea box of typically Irish almond oval shape with silvered copper mounts and cut into flat geometric patterns, *c.*1790.

19. *(bottom left)* An ormolu mounted tea caddy cut with diamond patterns and flutes English, *c.*1810.

20. *(bottom right)* Oval cut-glass caddy with silver-gilt mounts, English, *c.*1815.

3.   Enamel

ALLIED to glass, for it is a vitreous substance fused to a metal surface, enamel was used for bottle-shaped tea caddies made both in China (for export to Europe) and in England during the 18th century. Canton enamel, in which the opaque glass was fused on to a copper base, was painted with characteristic oriental flowers and symbols, often in the *famille rose* palette. Alternatively, a landscape or figure scene, sometimes derived from a European print,

21. An octagonal Canton enamel tea caddy with a silver cover, decorated with flower scrolls on a blue ground and with a mountainous landscape in leaf-shaped cartouches, Chinese, mid-18th century, 5¾in. high.

22. A set of two Birmingham enamel tea caddies and a sugar canister painted with flowers, c.1754, 3½in. high.

23. Set of three canisters transfer-printed and painted in puce monochrome on white enamel with farming and pastoral scenes and classical landscapes, contained in a blue aventurine glass casket with gilt-metal mounts, Birmingham, c.1770–75.

24. Late 18th century Staffordshire enamel tea caddy with powder blue ground heightened in gilt and painted all over with a diaper pattern of flowerheads, with ripple moulded mounts and chased gilt bronze handle.

may be found on a tea caddy (fig. 21).

A similar technique was used in England at Battersea and in South Staffordshire for decorating candlesticks, scent bottles, small boxes and other objects, including tea caddies, in the second half of the 18th century. They are gaily painted with flowers, landscapes, figure compositions and birds, sometimes following contemporary printed designs, and were much exported to the Continent. Most are of a rectangular box shape with a narrow cylindrical neck and round cover (figs. 22 and 23). Sets of enamel canisters of this type, each comprising a pair of round-necked tea caddies and a lidded sugar box fitted into a matching enamel tea chest, were made from the 1750s. Enamel boxes of oval shape and similar decoration are generally recognized as tobacco jars, owing to the loose press which is found in some of them. It is possible, however, that some were made as tea caddies, especially later in the 18th century (fig. 24).

4. Silver and Other Metals

FROM the early 18th century onwards, silversmiths provided some of the most richly fashionable tea caddies. At first the shapes of these were based on the Chinese red stoneware tea jars imported from the late 17th century onwards: they were globular or octagonal, with closely fitting caps over short cylindrical necks. Although at least one silver tea caddy is known from the late 17th century (an example by James Cockburn of Edinburgh, c.1685) the earliest, generally speaking, date from the reign of Queen Anne (fig. 25).

It was not long before the shapes of silver tea caddies began to develop along their own lines and, in turn, to influence those of other materials, and this trend continued for the next half-century. The typical style of the 1720s and 30s was a plain rectangular box with cylindrical neck and domed cap; some-

25. An octagonal silver tea caddy of small size by Glover Johnson, London, 1713, 5⅜in. high.

26. A set of three silver canisters engraved with coats of arms and with slide on covers, the two outer canisters also with slip-on caps, made by James Smith, London 1730, 4¾in. high.

27. A pair of tea caddies and a sugar box, the caddies each with a sliding base and domed cover chased with a sunflower, made by Samuel Taylor, 1750.

28. A set of three
rectangular canisters by
Pierre Gillois, London,
1768, decorated with
engraved flowers and foliage
with a coat of arms and
crests, fitted in a silver-
mounted shagreen case.

29. A set of tea caddies with
a sugar box, cream jug, 12
teaspoons, mote spoon,
sugar nippers, a pair of
pistol-handled knives with
detachable steel blades, in a
silver-mounted mahogany
box, made by Paul de
Lamerie, 1735.

times armorial or other decoration was engraved on the fronts, and there was usually a
sliding panel either in the top or in the base of
each tea canister so that it could be filled easily
(fig. 26).

It had now become the custom to produce
silver canisters in sets of three (see page 7)
and most of them were fitted into elegant
boxes, of wood, tortoiseshell or shagreen
which could be locked (figs 27, 28 and 33).
Sometimes such a set also included sugar nips
and spoons fitted into velvet-lined compartments inside or secreted in the lid or base of
the chest itself by means of small sliding panels
(fig. 29).

30. Set of three caddies by Thomas Gilpin, London, 1742–45.

31. A pair of silver caddies and a sugar box with rococo decoration; one caddy and the sugar box by Aymé Videau, London 1749 and one caddy by Samuel Taylor, London 1756.

Both the shapes and decoration of silver tea canisters grew more elaborate as the century progressed: the plain dome-topped ovals and rectangular box-like shapes with restrained floral or armorial decoration were beginning to give way to highly fanciful rococo designs by the 1750s. Asymmetrical cartouches were chased with chinoiseries, figure scenes, landscapes or coats of arms; shells, gadroons, flowers, flourishes of acanthus and festoons were embossed and engraved over the entire surfaces of tea boxes (figs. 30, 31, 32 and 102). A rectangular bombé form became highly fashionable in mid-century and a new lightness of effect was achieved with pierced and

32. Set of bombé shaped canisters engraved with crests and chased with festoons of flowers, scrolls and foliage, and with strawberry buttons on the lids, by Daniel Smith & Robert Sharp, London, 1761.

33. A tea caddy set by Samuel Taylor, London, 1761, with chinoiserie chasing typical of the period 1760–65, and with their original shagreen case.

34. *(below)* A shaped oval tea caddy engraved with bright-cut floral festoons, scrolls and so on with a domed lid and green stained ivory pineapple finial, by Henry Chawner, London 1786.

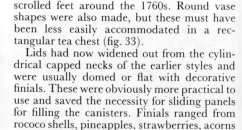

scrolled feet around the 1760s. Round vase shapes were also made, but these must have been less easily accommodated in a rectangular tea chest (fig. 33).

Lids had now widened out from the cylindrical capped necks of the earlier styles and were usually domed or flat with decorative finials. These were obviously more practical to use and saved the necessity for sliding panels for filling the canisters. Finials ranged from rococo shells, pineapples, strawberries, acorns and flowers to Chinese figures, putti or birds. Some were hinged so they could be laid flat when stored in a chest (figs. 30 and 31).

It is likely that most domestic silversmiths

included tea caddies among their wares, but some, such as Samuel Taylor, were noticeably prolific. Another, Pierre Gillois, working mainly in the third quarter of the century, was evidently a specialist, for almost all his surviving work consists of tea caddy and sugar box sets, some of the highest quality (fig. 28).

The neoclassical period of the 1770s onwards heralded a return to plainer shapes and more restrained decoration. Simple oval, cube-shaped and rectangular caddies with two inside compartments and their own locks and keys were engraved with delicate borders or symmetrical bright-cut patterns of garlands of flowers or ribbons (fig. 34).

Silver tea caddies following the contemporary design styles of the time were produced throughout the 19th century, and by some eminent silversmiths, but not in such large

35. A six-sided neoclassical tea caddy on three ball feet, made in London in 1808 by Thomas Holland, 5in. high.

36. An unusual silver caddy with two handles, made by J. Angell, London, 1845.

37. A set of three early Sheffield plate caddies embossed in the rococo taste, c.1760.

38. One of a pair of Sheffield plate tea caddies of oval form and with neoclassical decoration, c.1775.

numbers as before. The age of the silver tea caddy was virtually over (figs. 35 and 36).

Silver plate on copper was used for tea caddies at least from the 1760s. Craftsmen working in London, Nottingham and Birmingham as well as Sheffield, made caddies of similar shape and decoration to the more expensive silver examples. Many of these old Sheffield plate caddies are fine examples of late 18th century decorative art in their own right (figs. 37, 38 and 39).

Other metal canisters and caddies included oriental silver and gilt metal examples from the East, especially China, imported during the 18th century. Exceptionally, a set of canisters or a single caddy of silver-gilt may appear on the art market.

The Imperial Russian small-arms factory at Tula produced jewel-like tea caddies of polished and cut steel in the neoclassical period of the late 18th century. Usually embellished with other materials such as ivory or with painted medallions, these are extremely rare (fig. 40). Faceted steel beads were also occasionally used for decorating tea caddies made in England in the same period, particularly as frames for Wedgwood jasper plaques and as decorative patterns on ivory examples (fig. 2).

39. A pair of Sheffield plate tea caddies of oval bellied form with flutes, and stained ivory finials, *c*.1805.

40. Russian tula-work tea caddy decorated with ivory, enamels and miniature paintings in oval medallions, *c*.1775.

5. Wood

41. A Queen Anne period walnut tea chest with brass mounts.

42. 'Six Designs of Tea Chests' from Chippendale's *Director*, showing the rococo style fashionable in the 1760s.

WOODEN tea chests and caddies which form the majority of all tea containers, provide a history of 18th and 19th century cabinet-making techniques in microcosm, and because the tea equipage so often represented a status-enhancing luxury many tea boxes were made to the highest standards of craftsmanship and in the period's most exotic timbers. Wood could be carved, inlaid, veneered with marquetry or painted, and wooden frameworks could be japanned or covered with other materials – tortoiseshell, ivory, mother-of-pearl, curled paper, leather or even porcupine quills. There was hardly a technique known to 18th and 19th century craftsmen that was not used in the making and embellishing of tea chests and caddies either wholly or partly of wood. Tea chests not only feature in many of the lists of items made by the 18th century London furniture makers but

Six Designs of Tea Chests -   Nº CLIX

T. Chippendale inv. et delin.   Published according to Act of Parliament 1762.   W. Foster sculp.

43. Mahogany tea chest with gadroon border, c.1760.

44. Mahogany tea chest with ivory escutcheon, c.1760.

they are to be seen illustrated on some of their trade cards, which suggests that tea chests ranked among the cabinet-makers' most prestigious wares.

The earliest wooden tea chests date from the reign of Queen Anne and most are of walnut, but few survive from before the mid-18th century (fig. 41). At this time the casket-shaped tea chest had two or three compartments inside. Black and green tea would be kept in foil-lined lidded sections on either side, or in removable boxes of wood, silver or other metal. Sometimes there was a third box or partition for sugar (see page 8). Occasionally a concealed sliding section in the lid or base of

45. Selection of wooden tea caddies showing painting *(top row, centre)*, marquetry, herringbone and chequered bandings *(bottom row, centre and right)*, and some of the many shapes typical of late 18th and early 19th century examples.

Tea Chests.

Plans

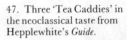

Tea Caddies

Plans.

47. Three 'Tea Caddies' in the neoclassical taste from Hepplewhite's *Guide*.

tea chest secreted a caddy spoon, mote spoon or the key – for all of them had locks.

Chippendale published 'Six Designs of Tea Chests' in the *Gentleman & Cabinet-Maker's Director* (third edition, 1762): they are all in the fashionable rococo style and were probably taken as models by many tea chest makers during the next decade or so (fig. 42). At this time, mahogany was most often used and carved decoration on the corners and feet might be enhanced with elaborate brass or silver handles and escutcheons (fig. 43). Some were decorated with cast metal mounts on the corners, as well as handles, feet and keyholes. Plainer examples, many of them no less finely made, sometimes had inlaid ivory escutcheons which contrasted elegantly with the rich dark ones of figured mahogany (fig. 44).

Never was there more diversity of shape,

48. *(top left)* An inlaid and crossbanded satinwood tea caddy, *c.*1780.

49. *(top right)* An oval harewood tea caddy with marquetry flowers and borders, *c.*1780.

50. *(bottom left)* A mahogany caddy crossbanded with calamander, *c.*1800.

51. *(bottom right)* A burr yew tea caddy with shallow pointed lid, *c.*1780.

52. Plain mahogany single-compartment caddy with boxwood stringing and a patera inlaid in the lid, *c*.1780.

material or decoration than on the tea caddies of the last quarter of the 18th century and the first decade of the 19th. The word 'caddy' (see page 7) now became associated with the smaller, often single-compartment, containers of square, oval, round or multi-sided form which began to be produced in great numbers from the 1770s onwards (fig. 45).

In *The Cabinet-Maker and Upholsterer's Guide* (1788) Hepplewhite published designs for three 'Tea Chests' (with three compartments) and three 'Tea Caddies' (figs. 46 and 47). He suggests that 'The ornaments may be inlaid with various coloured woods, or painted and varnished.' Perhaps following his advice, a Cornish cabinet-maker, John Best of St Columb, advertised 'plain, inlaid and varnished, tea caddies' on his trade label around the turn of the century.

Besides mahogany of many hues, satinwood was much favoured for tea caddies, but fruitwood, harewood (dyed sycamore), burr yew, amboyna, ebony, coromandel and rosewood were among the other timbers used (figs. 48, 49, 50 and 51). The plainest caddies were usually square or rectangular, with no more

53. Mahogany double-compartment caddy with herringbone stringing and inlaid burr-wood decoration, *c*.1785.

31

54. *(above)* An octagonal
sycamore tea caddy with
chequer stringing and
marquetry decoration in
satinwood and tulipwood,
mounted with a silver
handle and escutcheon
dated 1789.

55. *(right)* Two late 18th
century marquetry tea
caddies showing typical
decoration of the period.

56. Octagonal double-
compartment satinwood tea
caddy decorated in
marquetry typical of the late
18th century.

than a stringing of holly or box along the edge
for decoration (fig. 52). Others had cross
banding of more exotic woods, or herringbon
and chequered border patterns. Keyhole
were most often of a pale wood or of ivory (figs
53 and 54).

Marquetry decoration ranged from simpl
shells or paterae in contrasting woods t
elaborate floral and even architectural com
positions (figs. 55, 56 and 57). Some employe
only two or three different types of venee
while others used as many as half a dozen fo
maximum effect. Such motifs as shells, birds
ribbons, palms, paterae and so on, as well a
patterned strips of moulding, could be pur
chased ready-made from trade suppliers, an
according to the *Cabinet-Makers' London Book o
Prices* (1793) the price of 'Letting in an oval o

shell three inches long' on a plain square caddy costing 2s. 3d. was an extra 2d. Cross-bandings, lining the inside with lead instead of tin foil, dovetailing the carcase instead of nailing, or 'brading' it together, and 'lining the bottoms with cloth' were all extras, and 'If the caddies are veneer'd with king, tulip, yew, snake or any other hard wood, to be extra in the shilling on the start price . . . 1½d.'

The *Cabinet-Makers' London Book of Prices* was compiled 'for the convenience of Cabinet-Makers in general: whereby the price of executing any piece of work, may be easily found' and is a useful guide to the kinds of cabinet wares in common production in the late 18th century. Besides the simple square caddy 'Four inches and a half long' the book gives priced details for 'A Square Double Caddy, seven inches and a half long . . . A Veneer'd Hexagon Caddy, six inches and a half long . . . A Veneer'd octagon caddy five inches long . . . A pointed circular Double Caddy eight inches long . . . An Oval Tea Chest eight inches and a half long,' and six others. Prices ranged from the 2s. 3d. already mentioned for the plain square caddy, or 2s. 9d. for a simple veneered hexagon, to £1 4s.

57. *(left)* A marquetry tea caddy decorated with designs of famous English ruins taken from Buck's *Antiquities* (1774).

58. *(right)* A satinwood tea chest with bandings of tulipwood and harewood, fitted with two canisters and a cut glass bowl, 18 silver teaspoons, a caddy spoon and sugar tongs, *c.*1810.

59. *(below)* A late 18th century painted caddy.

60. A late 18th century caddy with burr wood reserves and garlands of flowers composed of spots of holly or boxwood, characteristic of the style of an anonymous maker.

61. A group of 18th century fruit-shaped caddies including a cantaloup, apples, a pear and an oriental aubergine (*front right*).

for an oval tea chest. Extras could bring the price for this up to £1 15s. or more.

Among the more elaborate caddies from the late 18th century, vase and urn shapes, perhaps designed to complement knife cases of similar form, have been noted. Others had unusual fittings within, like the fine satinwood chest in fig. 58 with its set of teaspoons arranged round the sugar bowl. Very occasionally, a wooden tea caddy in the shape of a building turns up.

Painted wooden tea caddies of the late 18th century are among the most charming. They are decorated with flower borders, garlands and posies or, more ambitiously, with pastoral and figure compositions, and many were the work of amateurs (figs. 45 and 59).

Late 18th century and Regency period caddies of plain woods were sometimes decorated with applied prints. These included views of resorts and beauty spots, and figure compositions like those of Angelica Kauffmann or Adam Buck. They were a form of souvenir ware, inexpensive compared with most other kinds of tea caddies.

Common decorative characteristics have been identified in some groups of tea caddies, and while they can almost never be attributed to specific makers, one may recognize an

62. Selection of fruit tea caddies including *(top)* a rare pineapple, melons, pears and apples, and several painted examples, *c.*1790–1810.

63. Two early 19th century German fruit caddies with iron escutcheons.

anonymous craftsman's style. Certain border patterns recur on similarly shaped caddies made to set off paper filigree decoration (see page 41) and the work of another hand can be discerned in a group of small caddies each with reserve panels of burr wood surrounded by stylized garlands whose flower heads are composed of round spots of white holly or boxwood (fig. 60).

A popular type of tea caddy in the late 18th century, and one of the most sought-after by 20th century collectors, was the fruit form, turned in fruitwoods of various kinds. These were made in England and Germany, almost certainly in imitation of Chinese models, from the 1780s until well into the 19th century. Oriental examples from earlier in the 18th century are still to be found. They usually take the form of pears or aubergines and the stalks and outer leaves in contrasting dark woods unscrew to reveal tight-fitting inner lids. Their quality is of a fineness unmatched by the European examples they inspired (fig. 61). The most usual of these are apples and pears, but cantaloups, aubergines, and even strawberries and pineapples may be found (fig. 62). Some have painted effects but most are merely polished or varnished. Their hinged lids generally lift by means of a stalk or button-like

64. Mahogany sarcophagus shaped tea chest of c.1815.

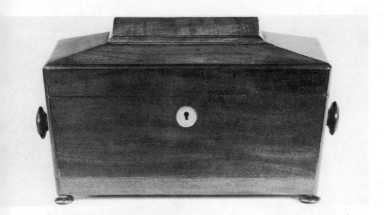

knob, and are quite loose-fitting. Their insides are lined with foil which, in genuine old examples, is now somewhat perished.

The key-hole escutcheons in late 18th century fruits are of steel, or silver for the best quality examples; brass for those made during the Regency period, and iron for the later 19th century fruits made in Germany. These are, besides, less finely made than those of the earlier period (fig. 63).

Throughout the Regency period and beyond, that is, from about 1810–35, the sarcophagus shape so beloved of the 19th century neoclassicists reigned supreme. It was eminently suitable for the larger casket-like tea chests which were favoured once again, and was interpreted in a host of different ways (figs. 64, 65, 66, 70 and 91). Rosewood now ranked with mahogany among the most popular cabinet-making woods and it was often embellished with brass or mother-of-pearl inlays. Gilded lion-mask and ring handles and paw feet enhanced the importance of some of these chunky chests, while others had elegant turned knobs and bun feet of matching wood or of ivory. Exotic burr woods like yew, amboyna and bird's eye maple were much favoured, and so were decorative effects like Tunbridge mosaic or penwork.

65. Sarcophagus shaped mahogany caddy with mother-of-pearl escutcheon, c.1820.

66. Amboyna tea chest of sarcophagus shape, with lion-mask handles and paw feet.

67. An early 19th century tea chest decorated with the type of parquetry sometimes associated with Tunbridge souvenir wares, *c*.1810.

68. A shaped double caddy with Tunbridge mosaic decoration depicting Eridge castle on the lid, with floral banding; the feet are of stickwork, *c*.1860.

Various kinds of souvenir woodwares had been produced in Tonbridge and Tunbridge Wells in Kent during most of the 18th century; these included fine parquetry work and, later, mosaic work in which sticks of variously coloured woods were glued together to form pictures and patterns, cut into slices and glued on to boxes and small objects of all kinds. Tunbridge mosaic was produced from the late Regency period onwards, and was copied elsewhere (figs. 67 and 68).

Penwork was a type of painting in black and white which was originally conceived as a cheap substitute for the elaborate and expensive ivory-inlaid furniture imported from India during the 18th century. Small furniture

69. A penwork tea chest with chinoiserie decoration.

70. Sarcophagus-shaped tea caddy with profuse and finely painted penwork decoration touched here and there with gold highlights.

and boxes of all kinds were embellished with 'Indian' designs of flowers and foliage, oriental figures and buildings, neoclassical scenes or flowers, generally in white on a lustrous black ground. Penwork was soon adopted as a pastime by ladies of an artistic fancy, and its popularity lasted for at least 50 years (figs. 69, 70 and 105).

Among the most popular souvenir wares from the 1820s to the 1850s were the pen-and-ink decorated boxes and the tartan wares of Mauchline in Scotland. Tea caddies of light sycamore bearing painted or transfer-printed views of well-known resorts, and/or covered in all-over tartan decoration may be found.

Towards the end of the Regency period,

71. *(left)* An interesting
rarity in the development of
the teapoy: a carved
mahogany tea chest
(originally containing a set
of three silver caddies)
supported by its original
stand with matching carved
paw feet, *c.*1810.

72. *(right)* George IV period
rosewood teapoy with four
caddies and spaces for two
bowls, its carcase decorated
with brass inlay and
supported on a lyre base.

an even larger tea container than the
sarcophagus-shaped chest was to be found in
fashionable drawing rooms. This was the
teapoy, a pillar-supported box which might
contain as many as four tea canisters. This
item of furniture developed, rather con-
fusingly, from a small side table popular in the
early 19th century: the word teapoy originally
had nothing to do with tea but was derived
from a Hindu word, *tepai*, meaning three-
legged or three-footed. Its transformation into
a teabox on legs (often a tripod) must have
seemed inevitable (figs. 71 and 72).

73. The back view of a hexagonal tea caddy decorated with coloured and gilded paper filigree.

I N 1786 the *New Lady's Magazine* referred to paper filigree work in glowing terms: 'The Art affords an amusement to the female mind capable of the most pleasing and extensive variety, it may be readily acquired and pursued at very trifling expense.' This art, of curling, twisting, rolling and crinkling strips of coloured paper and gluing them, end-on, into designs was an immensely popular pastime in the last quarter of the 18th century. Young girls at school were taught the skill and magazines of the period published designs for amateurs to copy. The *New Lady's Magazine* advertised 'A profusion of neat elegant patterns and models of ingenuity and delicacy suitable for tea-caddies, toilets, chimney-pieces, screens, cabinets, frames, picture ornaments etc' and publications such as *The Guiding Assistant to Paper Filigree Work* by C. Styart must have been helpful to those unable to procure the services of professional teachers.

74. Rolled paper tea caddy decorated by the famous locksmith, Joseph Bramah.

75. Elliptical tea caddy decorated with filigree patterns and garlands in curled paper.

76. Filigree paper caddy of hexagonal shape decorated with a posy of flowers tied with a bow and with wheatears.

The major vehicle for these fancy paper workers was the tea caddy, and large numbers of examples survive, some executed with astonishing skill, and others clearly the fumbling efforts of beginners (figs. 73 and 74). Special boxes and caddies of mahogany or satinwood with recessed frames, often edged with herringbone stringing, were made by the cabinet makers of the time and sold to filigree enthusiasts with appropriate coloured papers and, presumably, the metal ring handles with which most of them are surmounted. The *Cabinet-Makers' London Book of Prices* (1793) mentions caddies 'made for fillagree' and in 1791 Charles Elliott, the royal cabinet-maker, supplied Princess Elizabeth, daughter of George III with fifteen ounces of coloured filigree papers, one ounce of gold and a box made for filigree work with ebony mouldings, lock and key, lined inside and out, and 'a tea caddé to correspond with the box'. Another cabinet maker, Crowther of Halifax, adver-

77. Hexagonal rolled paperwork caddy with panels of stylized leaves and flowers, inset with a stipple engraving of a child at play, *c*.1800.

tised on his trade card 'Boarding Schools Supplied with Cases for Filligree Work on very reasonable terms.' Papers for filigree were also supplied by retailers of artists' materials like Ackermann in the Strand, but some ladies prepared their own.

Tea caddies were decorated with swirls and curlicues, neoclassical garlands, urns and anthemion borders; with bows, wheat-ears, birds and, above all, flowers (figs. 75 and 76). Single florets were coaxed out of round or oblong rolls of coloured paper, or pinched from ellipses; flowers were arranged into colourful borders, posies and even baskets and vases, usually against a regular background of tiny rolls. In many cases, a curled paper pattern was formed round a central cartouche with a miniature painting, print or embroidery let into it (fig. 77); very occasionally such a medallion was initialled by the maker and dated, giving it an especially valuable identity.

78. Oval tea caddy decorated entirely with gilt paper filigree.

79. A late 18th century paper filigree tea caddy with its original mahogany protective case.

80. A rolled paper tea caddy of elongated hexagonal form with two inset medallions and the decoration protected by glass panels, c.1790.

Some paper filigree designs do not cover the entire surface of a box, but form a raised pattern on a silk or glistening mica-strewn background. In others paper strips of different widths have been used to create a relief effect. In most cases the colours have faded to a pleasing mellowness but gilding has often survived to give a rich appearance. Some caddies were apparently decorated entirely with gilt-edged papers, perhaps to simulate the metal filigree from which the craft was derived (fig. 78). A few were covered only in white paper curls, resulting in an ivory-like appearance. The best preserved paperwork caddies are the rare examples with their own protective outer cases (fig. 79); the colours in these are usually as brilliant as when they were first made. Some caddies had panels of glass covering the curled paperwork designs, and these also tend to remain in good condition even if their colours have faded (fig. 80).

Tortoiseshell

VENEERS of tortoiseshell (on a wooden base) were used to decorate some of the most sumptuous tea caddies from the late 18th century onwards. Because of the small size of the average tortoiseshell plate it is rare to find the material used for veneering continuous surfaces and the earliest tortoiseshell tea caddies were most often of the single compartment type, often multi-sided and with shallow pointed or flat lids. Their facets were divided by fillets of creamy ivory (figs. 2 and 81). Simple square shaped caddies might rely solely on the flame-like mottling of the tortoiseshell for their decorative interest (fig. 82) or they might be enriched with finely patterned silver mounts and handles (fig. 83).

81. Tortoiseshell veneered tea caddy of octagonal shape with ivory fillets and silver mounts, *c*.1780.

82. Plain tortoiseshell caddy of *c*.1780.

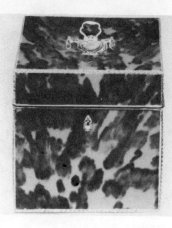

83. *(left)* A late 18th century square caddy veneered in scarlet tortoiseshell banded in silver and with a chased lambrequin handle plate.

84. *(right)* A late 18th century decagonal tea caddy veneered in tortoiseshell with ivory fillets and decorated with dots of mother-of-pearl.

84a. *(below)* Late Georgian tortoiseshell tea caddy, with mother-of-pearl floral inlay, standing on silver-plated ball feet.

As well as the natural brown colour of tortoise shell, tones of red, yellow and even green were achieved with coloured foil backing or with staining.

Tiny beads of pearl shell might be inlaid in patterns on a tortoiseshell surface in the late 18th century (fig. 84), and by the 19th more daring and elaborate mother-of-pearl inlays were being attempted. By this time the tea caddy was customarily of the larger casket shape, with two or three interior sections, and tortoiseshell examples inlaid with garlands and posies of engraved mother-of-pearl flowers are to be found (fig. 84a). Others have decorative motifs of silver inlaid by the *piqué posé* technique. These are usually further complemented by silver ball feet and surmounting knobs. Most of these larger caddies were not faceted like those of the earlier period, but their veneers were laid on in sections, in symmetrically arranged patterns. (fig. 2).

LIKE tortoiseshell, ivory was an exotic and valuable material, used only for tea caddies of the highest quality. Most date from the last quarter of the 18th century and they are generally of small dimensions. Slivers of ivory of various sizes were used to cover the sides of multi-faceted caddies, many of them with shallow pointed lids (fig. 85). The ivory was applied in narrow strips sometimes divided by ebony or tortoiseshell lines, and sometimes fluted to create a sculptural effect

85. Two late 18th century ivory tea caddies with tortoiseshell lines and silver mounts including medallions for the owners' initials.

86. A late 18th century fluted ivory tea caddy with an inset medallion depicting a slave in chains. This is based on Josiah Wedgwood's 'slave medallion' made on behalf of the Slave Emancipation Society on whose committee he sat from 1787; made in black jasperware on a white ground his cameos were inscribed 'Am I not a man and a brother?'

87. *(below)* A decagonal ivory tea caddy with tortoiseshell line inlay, the top inset with mother-of-pearl and gold dot inlay and the front inlaid with an inset gold plaque inscribed 'P', a gold escutcheon and rim to a circular miniature painting depicting a river scene. The interior is divided into two compartments, their lids surmounted with mother-of-pearl flower head knobs, *c*.1790.

(fig. 86). Round or serpentine shapes, or octagonal tea caddies with concave corners were occasionally made in this way.

Most ivory caddies have silver handles and key-hole escutcheons, and many have an inset silver medallion for the owner's initials (fig. 85); in the very best examples these are of gold (fig. 87). Decoration may include gold or silver *piqué clouté*, that is, patterns of tiny gold or silver pinheads (figs. 85 and 87) or inset Wedgwood medallions; sometimes these are surrounded by cut-steel bead decoration (fig. 2). As in many other kinds of tea caddies a favourite form of embellishment was an inset miniature painting (fig. 87). Some ivory examples belong to a rare group in which the inset medallion depicts a Negro slave in

chains; these were evidently designed to
awaken polite drawing room consciences to
the anti-slavery movement (fig. 86).

From India came tea caddies of native
woods like coromandel or rosewood inlaid
with ivory flowers, or wooden boxes veneered
all over with engraved ivory. As well as the
characteristic stylized plant borders and
exotic flowery garlands, some of these Indian
ivory caddies are decorated with buildings or
even formed into the shapes of neat houses
with pitched roofs for lids. Others are of solid
ivory, carved and pierced (fig. 88). Among the
larger ivory tea chests are elaborate carved
Chinese export caskets. The finest date from
the 18th century and have European silver or
glass canisters within.

88. An 18th century Indian
carved and pierced ivory tea
chest.

9. Mother-of-Pearl

89. An 18th century oriental mother-of-pearl tea chest with silver mounts.

ELABORATELY carved oriental mother-of-pearl chests with silver mounts were imported into Europe in the second half of the 18th century (fig. 89). Many of them were fitted with English silver tea canisters.

While mother-of-pearl was used with great effect for the decoration of English tortoiseshell tea caddies from the late 18th century onwards, examples covered entirely with mother-of-pearl rarely date from before the late Regency period. They invariably consist of a wooden base covered with diamond-shaped or rectangular slivers of shell. In some, dark greenish blue shell has been used to make contrasting patterns with the pale creamy white, while in others, mottled tortoiseshell bandings enhance its pearly lightness (fig. 90).

90. Regency period mother-of-pearl tea caddy with tortoiseshell banding.

10. Lacquer and Japanning

THE exotic lacquer wares of the East, imported into Europe from the 17th century onwards, were much sought after but expensive, and it was not long before attempts were made to copy them. True oriental lacquer is made from the sap of a tree which cannot be grown in Europe and alternatives were found in the form of varnishes of various kinds which could be applied in a similar manner – layer upon layer, each laboriously rubbed down to a glassy smoothness. To differentiate it from oriental lacquer this European type is known as japanning, and it was popular in one form or another throughout the 18th century and for much of the 19th.

91. Regency period sarcophagus-shaped tea caddy japanned on a cream ground and fitted with ivory handles and feet.

Tea chests of oriental lacquer and of European japanning may be found, dating from the middle years of the 18th century. They are nearly always the outer protective cases for silver or glass tea canisters and may be of high quality with elaborate brass locks and feet. European examples are most often of black japanning with gold chinoiserie decoration (see front cover). Later chests dating from the 19th century and made both for export from China and in Europe, are more frequently encountered, and some japanned wooden tea chests of the Regency period are enhanced by elegant ivory handles and feet (figs. 91 and 92).

Japanning on metal was a technique developed in the Pontypool area of Wales in the early 18th century and subsequently practised there, and in Birmingham and Wolverhamp-

92. Mid-19th century Chinese export black and gold lacquer tea chest containing four pewter canisters.

ton, and on the Continent. From the second half of the 18th century onwards finely decorated tin-plate tea caddies were being produced, some with flowers or chinoiseries in colours and gilding and others with stylized motifs or coats of arms (fig. 93). Those made from the mid-19th century in the West Midlands for a mass market are not of such high quality as the earlier japanned tin wares but they are unpretentiously attractive and often colourful (fig. 94). Late 19th and early 20th century biscuit tins in the shapes of tea caddies are also worth consideration. They were produced by such firms as Huntley & Palmers, Peak Frean, Carr, MacFarlane Lang and others, and their popularity with collectors has led to a steep rise in prices during the past decade.

93. Regency period japanned tin tea chest with silvered mounts, containing two canisters and a space for a sugar bowl, decorated with chinoiseries on a red ground.

94. Mid-19th century West Midlands tin tea caddy with 'crystallized' decoration in yellow, and a brass finial and feet.

95. Papier mâché tea caddy with neoclassical decoration and gilt metal mounts.

11. Papier mâché

ATTEMPTS to improve the techniques of making papier mâché or 'paperware' and to explore the commercial possibilities of decorating it with japan varnishes were made by a number of Birmingham men from the 1740s onwards, and culminated in Henry Clay's patent of 1772 for 'making in paper high varnished panels . . . cabinets, book-cases, screens, chimney pieces, tables, tea-trays and waiters,' which marked the start of the great papier mâché industry centred on Birmingham and Wolverhampton.

Among the many 'Clay's ware' products of the last quarter of the 18th century and the

96. Late 18th century oval papier mâché tea caddy with white anthemion borders and bronze speckling.

early 19th were square, rectangular or oval tea caddies in black with restrained decoration in the neoclassical style. Simple line and dot borders in white or red, garlands painted *en grisaille*, classically draped figures or inset Wedgwood cameos were usual, occasionally with greenish bronze 'speckling' (figs. 95 and 96). In 1775 tea caddies from Clay's factory cost three guineas each, so they were among the most expensive (cf. the prices of wooden tea caddies, page 33).

During the second quarter of the 19th century further advances both in manufacturing techniques and methods of decoration led to the production of a greatly increased range and quality of decorative goods in papier mâché. Tea caddies of an ever glossier finish were finely painted with polychrome flowers, bordered with gilding and inlaid with pearl shell (figs. 97 and 98).

97. Papier mâché tea chest, impressed 'Jennens & Bettridge, Makers to the Queen', *c.*1840.

98. *(below)* Finely decorated papier mâché tea caddy with painted fruit on the lid and gilding round the sides, mid-19th century.

AMONG the more unusual materials used for making, or at least covering tea caddies are leather, straw and marble. Mid-18th century tea chests containing silver or glass tea canisters were sometimes covered in morocco or in the type of untanned leather known as shagreen or sharkskin. This had a rough granular surface and was generally dyed green or black (figs. 13, 28 and 33). There were specialist makers of these leather-covered cases and one of them, John Folgham, listed 'Canister Cases etc in Blue or Green Dog Skin, mounted in Silver, or Plain' among his

99. Red leather tea caddy with gilt brass mounts, with its original cut glass containers – a bowl and stoppered tea caddy, c.1810.

many wares in about 1760. Later, in 1802, Henry Robinson of Angel Court, Snow Hill is listed as a 'maker of shagreen and mahogany knife cases, tea caddies, etc.'

Leather tea chests were made to simulate piles of gold-tooled books. At least one late 18th century example is known containing three Bristol green glass tea bottles and stoppers. Red leather boxes with elaborate gilt metal mounts were fashionable during the Regency, and tea chests of this type are occasionally seen. Fig. 99 shows a good example with its original inside fittings – a stoppered cut glass tea bottle and sugar bowl.

Straw-work of the early 19th century has an interesting social history: most examples were produced by Napoleonic prisoners of war incarcerated in England, who made a number of artefacts from the few materials available to them – bone, straw, hair and small pieces of wood – in order to pay for their own upkeep. They were allowed to sell their products in local markets and some were lucky enough to secure commissions from local people. Crudely made wooden boxes, including tea caddies, were sometimes covered with patterns of straw made with great skill by using various colours of the natural material laid in different directions to create contrast effects, and cutting short lengths into flower, leaf and other shapes. As well as naturalistic plants and garlands, mosaic patterns and scenes of buildings or ships were made (fig. 100).

Very occasionally tea caddies decorated in a colourful patchwork of marble diamonds, enriched with gilt metal mounts and feet, appear. They were made during the late Regency period, from the many coloured marbles found in Derbyshire.

100. Straw-work tea caddy made by French prisoners of war, c.1800.

13. Collecting

FAR from providing a new field for exploration, tea caddies have been popular with collectors for generations. Queen Mary was perhaps the most famous, and she left a number of treasures to the Victoria and Albert Museum where they can now be seen. Although no other museum collection in Britain has so many, most major museums in the British Isles have at least a sprinkling of tea caddies on view.

Because they are so widely collected tea caddies are rarely among the most obvious bargains, either in antique shops or the saleroom. On the other hand, one generally gets what one pays for, and a high price should secure an item of high quality, rarity and beauty.

101. Reproduction tea caddy in Adam style, *c*.1940.

Tea caddies have been reproduced and faked and some of these non-antiques are now old enough to be convincing; others will always reveal their true colours to the experienced eye (fig. 101). Some, for example those made in porcelain by Samson of Paris, are now collectors' items. Others, like some fruit-shaped caddies, may masquerade as 18th century examples when in fact they were made much later. Many tea caddies and chests have been subject to alteration and over-restoration if not actual vandalism. Collectors must be aware of all these possibilities and exercise extreme vigilance when searching. Opportunities to look at and handle tea caddies, and to talk about them with knowledgeable dealers and others should never be wasted.

Prices vary enormously, and they are governed as much by quality and rarity as by the material used. Among the most expensive are likely to be sets of silver caddies of early or mid-18th century period. A matching pair of caddies and a sugar box are always likely to fetch in excess of £1,000, but examples by well known makers may be much more expensive. A magnificent set of rococo caddies by Paul Crespin for example (fig. 102) were sold for £18,360 in 1983. But this was exceptional.

102. Set of three silver caddies by Paul Crespin, 1750, elaborately chased with chinoiserie figures and landscape panels within scroll and shellwork borders, and with flower finials. They were sold at Christie's in 1983 for £18,360.

103. An unusual double-compartment silver caddy made by Henry Nutting, 1803. An example of this quality could cost between £1000 and £2000.

Between £2,000 and £4,000 should secure a set of 18th century caddies of good quality.

Single silver canisters or caddies will normally range from about £400–£2,000, depending on quality and on the maker's name (fig. 103). Late 19th or early 20th century ones may be had for £100 or less and still be attractive Old Sheffield plate is much in demand by collectors and caddies dating from the 1760–1800 period will also command quite high prices. Between £800 and £1200 would not be unusual for a pair of neoclassical examples.

The best porcelain and enamel caddies will be in a similarly high-priced range to silver, but much will depend on condition, and the presence or loss of original covers makes an enormous difference to prices. The fine Meissen octagonal caddy of fig. 3 was sold for £7,150 in 1983, and although this was an especially splendid piece it is usual for lidded Meissen caddies to fetch in excess of £1000. Absence of a lid may reduce a price to £500 or £600. Worcester porcelain caddies dating from the second half of the 18th century are likely to fall into the £300–£800 bracket, depending on the rarity of the pattern, and examples from the German hard-paste factories like Frankenthal, Ludwigsburg and so on will be priced around £700–£800. Late 18th century Thuringian porcelain tea caddies, however, may be bought for between £100 and £200, and for less than £100 if their lids are missing. Blue and white porcelain caddies will be similarly priced.

It is virtually impossible to give price guidelines for pottery tea caddies, so variable are they in quality, condition and rarity. At one end of the scale one might pick up a blue and white pearlware example for as little as £30, while at the other a rare tin-glazed earthenware caddy could be as much as £2,000. Enamel caddies in sets are nearly always priced in excess of £700, but anyone lucky enough to find a trio of canisters in their original enamel casket would almost certainly have to pay at least £3,000 for them.

With any ceramic tea caddy condition is an important aspect: damage, as well as the lack of a cover, will reduce the value, and this consideration must be weighed up by anyone contemplating a purchase. Many people nowadays cannot afford to buy any but damaged pieces, and these can still bring enormous pleasure to the collector and enable his money to go further; some people, however, prefer to pay a good deal more for a perfect example, feeling that its value is more likely to rise consistently in the future. Much depends on the collector's motives: if the purpose is purely to enjoy living with his treasures, a small amount of damage need not matter. If on the other hand investment is the primary concern, good condition is more important.

The greatest variations probably occur in the prices of wooden tea caddies. Simple square or rectangular caddies of the late 18th

104. A rare ebony veneered tea chest with ivory fillets and inset on the front, sides and back with six Liverpool or Birmingham enamel plaques, transfer-printed in black. That on the front left shows *The Tea Party* engraved by Robert Hancock in the 1750s. This chest was probably made *c.*1760 and it fetched £1210 at Sotheby Parke Bernet in 1982.

105. Penwork tea chest decorated with flowers, late Regency period.

century, and less elaborate examples of th
Regency sarcophagus shape can be picked u
for around £50, and less if restoration
needed. Unfortunately many wooden caddi
have lost their inside fittings, and this aga
will reduce their value.

Wooden tea caddies of high quality, or
exotic veneers will command the high price
currently in evidence for antique furnitur
and certain types will be especially expensiv
(fig. 104). The much sought-after 18th centur
fruit-shaped caddies, for instance, may chang
hands for between £400 and £1500 (canta
loups are usually the most expensive) whi
the later 19th century examples will comman
prices above £300. Filigree paper caddies no:
mally sell for between £200 and £400, b
exceptionally fine ones may reach more. Othe
interesting types are Tunbridge ware an
penwork and for these a collector must expec
to pay £200 and upwards for good example
(fig. 105).

Tortoiseshell and ivory caddies are usuall
of fine quality and most fetch prices in exces
of £400. Late 18th century ivory caddies ofte
command prices over £1000. Even such roug
guidelines as these can hardly be given for te
caddies of materials such as papier mâche
japanned tin, lacquer, leather, straw-wor
and so on.

Almost every tea caddy, of whateve
material, is unique and must be judged on it
own merits. These should include consider
ations of condition, quality, rarity and age a
well as aesthetic appeal. Only experience ca
tell one if a particular caddy is too highl
priced. On the whole, one should b
courageous enough to buy the best one ca
afford. A decision to spend what might seem a
the time a lot of money on something on
really likes is rarely regretted later.

Acknowledgements

The author and publishers would like to thank the following for permission to use the photographs in this book:

Apter-Fredericks, London 86; Armitage, London 28; Asprey & Co, London (*cover*), ?, 30, 44, 45, 48, 49, 50, 51, 53, 55, 60, 61, 64, 67, 69, 76, 78, 81, 82, 90, 95, 100, 105; H. C. Baxter & Son, London 96; H. Blairman & Sons, London 99; Bonhams 33; J. H. Bourdon-Smith, London 35, 36, 103; Christie's 27, 79, 102; Delomosne, London 10, 1, 12, 14, 15, 16, 17, 18, 19, 20; Derek Roberts Antiques, Tonbridge 68; Halcyon Days, London 77; R & J Jones, London 4, 5, 9; Klaber & Klaber, London 6, 22; Lawrence Fine Art, Crewkerne 84a; Mallett, London 40, 41, 43, 62, 85, 88, 89, 93; Paul Couts, Edinburgh 57; Pelham Galleries, London 73; Peter Francis, London 71; Phillips Auctioneers 24, 37, 38, 54, 58, 59, 83; Royal Academy of Arts, London 13; Royal Albert Memorial Museum, Exeter 84; Royal Pavilion, Brighton 72; Science Museum, London 74; S. J. Shrubsole, London 34, 39; Sotheby Parke Bernet 3, 26, 52, 63, 80, 104; Sotheby's, Pulborough 75; Spink & Son, London 21, 25, 31; Stair & Co., London 87; Tate Gallery 1; Temple Newsam House, Leeds 29; Twinings, Andover 56, 91; Wolverhampton Museums 7, 8, 23, 94, 98.

Index

Bold page numbers refer to illustrations